Australia's Neighbours

Laos

DISCOVER THE COUNTRY, CULTURE AND PEOPLE

Jane Hinchey

REDBACK publishing

First published 2019 by
Redback Publishing
PO Box 357 Frenchs Forest NSW 2086
Australia

www.redbackpublishing.com.au
orders@redbackpublishing.com.au

978-1-925860-68-9

Author: Jane Hinchey
Editor: Marianne Lindsell
Designer: Redback Publishing

Original illustrations © Redback Publishing 2019
Originated by Redback Publishing

Printed and bound in China

MIX
Paper from responsible sources
FSC www.fsc.org FSC® C020056

Acknowledgements
Abbreviations: l—left, r—right, b—bottom, t—top, c—centre, m—middle
We would like to thank the following for permission to reproduce photographs: (Images © shutterstock) p12b Dietmar Temps, p16 gg-foto, p18rm Adrian Baker, p20b Phonepaseth Keosomsak, p28b Chokniti Khongchum,p29t Chanchura Pratanrad, p29b Jody McIntyre https://flic.kr/p/7NrJcM

Every effort has been made to contact copyright holders of any material reproduced in this book. Any omissions will be rectified in subsequent printings if notice is given to the publisher.

NATIONAL LIBRARY OF AUSTRALIA
A catalogue record for this book is available from the National Library of Australia

Contents

Map of Laos

CHINA
CHINA
VIETNAM
MYANMAR (BURMA)
LAOS
THAILAND
CAMBODIA
VIETNAM
Phongsali
Luang Namtha
Muang Xay
Ban Houayxay
Xam Neua
Luang Prabang
Phonsavan
Sainyabuli
Vang Vieng
Muang Phôn-Hông
Pakxan
VIENTIANE
Thakhek
Savannakhet
Salavan
Sekong
Pakse
Attapeu
HANOI
BANGKOK
Beibu Gulf
Mekong
Black
Red
Thác Bà Lake
Yu Jiang
Nam Ou
Ho Song Da
Song Cau
Song Ma
Nam Sam
Song Ca
Nam Ngum
Nam Ngum Reservoir
Mae Nam Nan
Sirikit Reservoir
Nam Kading
Nong Han Lake
Ubonrat Reservor
Lam Pao Reservor
Xe Banghiang
Lam Nam Chi
Lam Nam
Sirithon Reservor
Xe Kong

Snapshot

Official name:	Lao People's Democratic Republic
Population:	6,961,210 (2018)
Capital:	Vientiane
Area:	237,955 square kilometres
Languages:	Lao (official), Hmong, Khmu, French
Main Religion:	Buddhism
Currency:	Kip
Highest point:	Phou Bia 2,820 metres

MAJOR SITES

- Luang Prabang
- Vang Vieng
- That Luang (the Great Stupa)
- Tad Fane Waterfall
- Kuang Si Falls
- 4000 Islands region
- Kong Lor Caves
- Wat Phu

Fun Facts

- Laos is home to the Khone Phapheng, Southeast Asia's largest waterfall.
- The oldest human fossil in Southeast Asia was found in a cave in North Laos.
- During the Vietnam War, the USA dropped two million tons of bombs on Laos; making it the world's most bombed country.
- The Thai and Lao languages are very closely related.

Meet the Neighbour: Laos

Laos is a landlocked country in Southeast Asia, bordered by Myanmar to the northwest, Cambodia and Vietnam to the east, Thailand to the west and China to the north. Despite having no coast, Laos consists of more water than land.

Australia and Laos have an important partnership, economic, diplomatic and development links. In 2005 the Australian Chamber of Commerce was the first international chamber of commerce in Laos and in 2017, Australia and Laos celebrated 65 years of diplomatic relations.

Laos is a poor country, with approximately 23% of its population living under the national poverty line. Australia provides Laos with millions of dollars in aid annually. In 2018-19, the Australian Government will provide an estimated $41.3 million in Official Development Assistance (ODA) to Laos.

In the 2016 census, 12,000 people in Australia identified themselves as having Lao ancestry and close to 10,000 were born in Laos. Laos is becoming a popular destination for Australian travelers.

In 2016-17, Australian aid to Laos supported many programs including:

- **Repairs to 636 classrooms in 389 schools.**
- **Giving 140,000 primary children mid-morning snacks or lunch.**
- **32 Australia Awards scholarships, including 22 female recipients.**
- **Training for 3,045 people, half of them women, in financial literacy.**
- **Helping to clear 180 hectares of UXO contaminated land.**

Fast Fact

Australia is one of only two countries that have a regular human rights dialogue with Laos.

At a Glance

System of Government and the King

Laos is a one-party socialist republic. The Lao People's Revolutionary Party (LPRP) is the only legal political party.

The head of government is the Prime Minister, who is elected by a National Assembly for a five-year term. Government policies are determined by the party through the 11-member Politburo of the Lao People's Revolutionary Party and the 61-member Central Committee. Important government decisions are vetted by the Council of Ministers.

The country is divided into 17 provinces and one municipality.

Economy

Major Industries:

Copper, tin, gold and gypsum mining; construction, garments, cement, tourism, timber, electric power and agricultural processing.

Main Agriculture:

Sweet potatoes, vegetables, corn, coffee, sugarcane, tobacco, cotton, peanuts and rice.

Main Exports:

Tin, copper, gold, wood products, garments, electricity and coffee. Laos's main export partners are the Thailand, China and Vietnam.

Main Imports:

Machinery and equipment, vehicles, fuel and consumer goods. Laos' main import partners are the Thailand, China and Vietnam.

Natural Resources:

Tin, gold, gemstones, gypsum, lead, zinc, coal, potash, iron ore and petroleum. Other resources include forests and potential hydro-electric power.

Into the Future

The government opened Laos to the world in the 1990s. Tourism is now the fastest growing industry and plays a vital role in the Lao economy.

The Most Heavily Bombed Country in the World

Laos has heavy contamination from cluster munition remnants. During the Vietnam War, the United States dropped two million tons of bombs on Laos; making it the world's most bombed country per capita ever. Millions of these bombs still litter the landscape undetonated. They often explode when accidentally struck by farmers, playing children or buffaloes. Huge areas of land remain unusable, which impacts agriculture, industry, tourism and the daily lives of the Lao people. It is estimated that there have been more than 25,000 victims of UXO since the war ended in 1973.

Finding and dismantling landmines is an expensive and laborious process. In Laos, the government works with various NGOs and private organisations to clear the land. So far, over 4.9 million square metres of land has been cleared, with over 35,000 explosive devices destroyed, improving the lives of over 9,000 local people.

The Ottawa Convention

The Ottawa Convention, or Mine Ban Treaty, is an international treaty that went into force on 1 March 1999 and stops the production and use of landmines. Since its inception, about 51 million anti-personnel mines have been removed from arsenals and destroyed. Despite 80% of the world's states already joining, the USA, China and Russia haven't.

Facts About Landmines

Landmines are explosive traps that detonate when they come into contact with a person or vehicle. Generally, they are scattered across an area or buried about 15 centimetres under the ground. There are 600 different types of landmines, grouped into two categories: anti-personnel landmines and anti-tank landmines. Anti-tank landmines are designed to destroy vehicles that drive over them. Anti-personnel landmines are triggered when they come into contact with a person, which has had serious ramifications for civilians. In affected areas, children, farmers, and women collecting water all become victims of this weapon of war. These deadly devices have killed hundreds of thousands of children who were herding animals, planting crops or just playing.

Frightening Facts:

- There are estimated to be around 110 million anti-personnel mines in the ground worldwide.
- Approximately 100 million mines are stockpiled around the world.
- One million people have been killed and maimed by anti-personnel mines.
- 70 people a day or 26,000 people annually are victims of landmines.
- Over 300,000 children are severely disabled because of landmines.
- Landmines are a serious problem in 76 countries and territories around the world, including Laos, Cambodia, Afghanistan, Iraq, Angola, Bosnia, Croatia, Sri Lanka, Myanmar and many more.
- The main producers of landmines are India, Myanmar, Pakistan and South Korea.
- A landmine costs around $3.70 to manufacture, but $1,250 to clear from an area.

People

Laos has a population of around 7 million people, making it one of the most sparsely populated countries in Asia. Two-thirds of the population live in rural areas, although urbanisation is steady. Vientiane is the largest city with a population of 562,244.

There are as many as 200 distinct ethnic groups in Laos, but since 2005 the Laos government only recognizes four broad categories, based on ethnic and linguistic similarities. More specifically, 240 subgroups of people have been divided into 49 ethnic groups, from which four ethno-linguistic groups have been categorised. The ethno-linguistic groups that make up Laos' current system are the Lao Tai, Mon-Khmer, Chinese Tibetan and Hmong Mien.

Lao Tais (Lao Loum)

The biggest ethnic group in Laos is the Lao Loum, the country's lowlanders. In this category, 23 ethnic groups are recognised, making up 87% of the population. They arrived from South China over 4,000 years ago.

Ethnic Groups– A Breakdown

Lao	53.2%
Khmu	11%
Hmong	9.2%
Phouthay	3.4%
Tai	3.1%
Makong	2.5%
Katong	2.2%
Lue	2%
Akha	1.8%
other	11.6%

Daily Life

Family is the focus of daily life and it's common for family to live with two or more generations. Most families are still involved in farming and retain traditional ways. Young people are expected to respect their elders and take care of them when they are old. The home is still the domain of the women and gender plays a role in the division of labour. On rice farms, men do work such as ploughing, controlling water, sowing and reaping the crop. Women weed and carry the sheaves of rice to the threshing place. Other chores that are split include hunting, the fetching of water and collection of forest food.

Life revolves around seasonal cycles and the Buddhist calendar.

Healthcare

Until recently, Laos' healthcare system has been rudimentary but more health programs have now been put in place. The government has prioritised a health strategy that aims to achieve equality in access to healthcare by 2020.

One major problem is that many people don't seek treatment immediately when they are sick, which means there has been a spread of infectious diseases. There is also an increase in tobacco and alcohol-related illnesses, illicit drug use and its related problems.

Some organisations are addressing the broader issues involved in maintaining good health, such as sanitation, clean water and nutrition.

Sport

Soccer is the most popular sport in Laos, although the national team is yet to make a major international competition. However, Laos was a founding member of the Southeast Asia Games and hosted them in December 2009.

Other popular sports include Thai style boxing, Muay Lao and Sepak Takraw, which is a mixture of volleyball and football.

The education system is currently under reform in Laos with the Education Sector Development Plan for 2016-2020. The ESDP 2016-20 also develops sporting opportunities.

The Arts

Laos has a rich history of traditional arts influenced heavily by exposure to nearby cultures, especially along the Mekong. Myanmar, Thai and Khmer influences are apparent. Regional and rural art forms include silverwork and goldwork, weaving and basket making, wood and ivory carving. Buddhism and Hinduism also play a large role in cultural and intellectual life, especially in local literature.

Music is made using instruments such as flutes, plucked and bowed lutes, drums, cymbals and the khene, a wood-and-bamboo mouth organ. Most music is passed from generation to generation as part of an oral tradition.

Muay Lao boxer at a traditional rural tournament in a village near Vientiane

Did You Know?

In Laos, the government controls all aspects of the media, including the press, broadcasting and the internet.

Clothes

The female traditional costume is the sinh, with similarities to traditional Thai and Cambodian costumes. It consists of a tube skirt made of silk, a blouse and a long embroidered sash that is draped across one shoulder. Unlike in Thailand where this clothing is worn for special events, many Laotian women still wear this daily.

The male traditional costume is a peasant pant called a salong.

Both the sinh and salong come in various colours depending on where they are worn, such as a wedding, funeral or festival.

Traditional Houses

Traditional homes in rural areas have wooden frames, thatched, tiled or iron roofs and walls of timber or woven bamboo. The houses are raised on stilts to help the flow of air and also protect from flooding. The area under the house is used to relax, keep cool, and to keep animals.

Language

There are 86 languages spoken in Laos. They belong to Mon-Khmer, Hmong-Mien and Sino-Tibetan language families besides other Tai-Kadai languages. Many people also speak French.

The official language is Lao, or Laotian, which has influenced the Khmer and Thai languages and vice versa. It is spoken by approximately 15 million people in Laos and Thailand. It is a tonal language. There are six tones for each word and each different tone changes the meaning of the word. There are no spaces between words. Spaces in a Lao text indicate the end of a clause or sentence.

Learn the Lingo

Yes	Jao
No	Baw
Maybe	Bangthi
Please	Khâluna
Thank you	Khop tchaï laï laï
Sorry/excuse me	Khãw thôht
Good morning / Good evening	Sabaï dii / None lap fan dii
How are you?	Sabaï dii bo?
Fine, thank you, and you?	Sabaï dii, khop tchaï, lè tchao dè?
I understand / I don't understand	Khaphachao khao tchaï / Khoï bo khao tchaï
I'm lost	Khoy lohng taang
Can you help me?	Suay khoy dai boh

Ministry of Education and Sports Education Sector Development Plan for 2016-2020

The Education Sector Development Plan for 2016-2020 (ESDP 2016-20) responds to the following priorities of the 8th NSEDP, specifically:

- Continue to expand the achievement of the implementation of National Education System Reform Strategy to become stronger at all levels and at post-basic education level to better respond to the demands of socio-economic development, particularly in remote areas through improved infrastructure, updated curriculum and improved quality of teaching and learning.
- Fulfil the policy on compulsory education at primary level and then at the lower secondary level as a foundation for the development and upgrading of labour skills and quality, ensuring incentives are applied to attract more students at vocational education level, particularly to produce graduates in the fields of electrical, mining, processing, handicraft, mechanics and services, to ensure a sufficient labour force for the production and services sectors in supporting future national development and enhance the capacity to integrate and compete at regional and international levels.
- Develop capacity for athletes to become professionals and gradually reach regional and international standards and to encourage all people to play sports and gymnastics, promoting and developing indigenous sports.

Education

School is compulsory and all children supposedly attend between the ages of six and fifteen. However, the reality is more complex. Laos is close to achieving universal access to primary education, with over 97% enrolment for primary school. However, dropout rates are high and there are still many hurdles to overcome, such as a lack of infrastructure and family issues which impact attendance at school for many children.

In many ethnic communities children find it difficult to learn in Lao, a language that is often not their mother tongue. Also, some communities believe education is for boys only. Children with special needs are rarely educated.

The Laotian government has universal education in mind for all its citizens and an education plan is now in place to overhaul the education system. The plan aims to help Laos move from being one of the world's least developed countries by 2020 and move to industrialisation and modernity.

Australia provides aid to support educational programs in Laos. Focus has been on constructing classrooms, training teachers and providing school meals, with recent emphasis on school management, teacher training and an improved curriculum.

Four-Step Plan

Congress highlighted four breakthrough steps, which were further developed into a plan that modernised education. The steps are:

- Advancements in ideology.
- Human resources development.
- Overcoming administrative barriers which impede business activities.
- Increasing efforts in poverty reduction.

Life in Cities

Most of Laos is still rural. City life is limited to Vientiane and some smaller provincial cities. Unlike other Asian cities where people have migrated to these urban areas looking for work, in Laos it is more financially viable to live in a rural area close to a city and provide produce for the city dwellers.

The largest city is the capital, Vientiane, located on the Mekong River. Founded in 1562, it now has 600,000 inhabitants. Unlike the capitals of neighbouring countries such as Thailand, Cambodia and Vietnam, Vientiane is still small. However recent rapid economic growth means the city has decent infrastructure, and tourism and foreign investment has brought with it a buzzing café and restaurant scene.

Generally, life in urban areas is laid back and crime is low. Traditionally, people live in homes made of wood, but apartment blocks are now common.

Largest Cities in Laos

	City	Population
1	Vientiane	562,244
2	Savannakhet	93,277
3	Pakxe	88,166
4	Thakhek	55,600
5	Muang Xai	52,267
6	Luang Prabang	51,203
7	Xam Neua	42,896
8	Phonsavan	37,507
9	Vang Vieng	25,000
10	Muang Pakxan	24,686

Life in Rural Areas

About 80% of Laos's population live in rural areas. Over 40% of these people live in poverty.

For those in rural communities, their way of life has not changed much for generations. Families still live in traditional style homes and own farms or small businesses. Many generations live under one roof. Villages can consist of a few families or hundreds of families. Homes cluster together with rice fields surrounding the village.

Most villagers have gardens and orchards and raise chickens, pigs or buffalo. Households are generally self-sufficient and raise their own food. Most villages have only basic public services.

Natural Disasters

The most common natural disasters to affect Laos are floods, droughts, earthquakes, cyclones, and infectious disease epidemics. The impacts of these disasters are especially felt in rural areas where economic livelihoods are reliant on agriculture.

In July 2018, part of a dam system collapsed killing 36 people. At least 98 people were missing and 6,600 others were displaced.

Timeline

7000 BC
People living in the area settle and begin farming.

900 AD
The Khmer empire expands into the northern and central regions.

14th Century AD
After the decline of the Khmer Empire, Fa Ngum founds the Kingdom of Lan Xang and Theravada Buddhism becomes the state religion.

1560
King Setthathirat moves the capital from Luang Prabang to Vientiane.

Statue of King Setthathirat at Pha That Luang

1637-94
The Golden Age of Lan Xang in Vientiane.

1893
Laos becomes a French protectorate.

1945
Laos is occupied by the Japanese towards the end of World War II.

1946
French rule over Laos is resumed.

1953
Laos gains full independence as a constitutional monarchy. Civil war breaks out between royalists and the communist group, the Pathet Lao.

1960s
The Communist government of North Vietnam begins extensive use of the Ho Chi Minh Trail in Laos. Laos is subjected to extensive bombing by the United States.

1973
A ceasefire agreement divides Laos between the communists and the royalists.

1975
The Pathet Lao overthrows the royalist Lao government and forces King Savang Vatthana to abdicate. The Lao People's Democratic Republic is established.

1993-94
The Friendship Bridge opens across the Mekong, linking Laos and Thailand. A new age begins, opening Laos up to tourism.

1997
Laos is admitted to the Association of Southeast Asian Nations (ASEAN).

2000
Laos celebrates 25 years of communist rule.

2006
Choummally Sayasone becomes president.

2009
Rail link with Thailand opened over the Mekong at Nong Khai.

2011
A new stock market opens in Vientiane.

2016
Bounnhang Vorachith is appointed as president and leader of the ruling Lao People's Revolutionary Party (LPRP), succeeding Choummaly Sayasone.

The Friendship Bridge over the Mekong

Religion and Beliefs

The government of Laos recognises four religions: Buddhism, Christianity, Islam and Bahai. The Constitution provides for freedom of religion.

Buddhism is the main religion in Laos, with most Lao practising Theravada Buddhism. Buddhists live by the Five Moral Precepts, which involve refraining from:

- Harming living things.
- Taking what is not given.
- Sexual misconduct.
- Lying or gossip.
- Taking intoxicating substances such as drugs or drink.

Animistic Paths

Many Lao people consult fortune-tellers and palmists. Astrologers are still consulted before making decisions about marriage or business and also to help choose auspicious days for major events.

Many young Lao men become monks for a period of time. Ordained Buddhist monks have 227 precepts they live by. Many of them are rules about behaviour, drinking and eating, and dressing.

Approximately 1% of Laos's population is Muslim and Bahai. There are two active mosques in the capital.

Overall, only 1.5 % of the population is Christian. There are both Protestant and Catholic Christians in Laos as well as a growing Evangelical movement.

Baci Ceremony

Baci is an important Lao custom where strings are tied around a person's wrist. Baci are held for both happy and sad occasions and to preserve good luck. Baci ceremonies can be held any day of the year, but elders and monks choose auspicious days on which to hold them.

During the ceremony, a white thread is tied on the right hand wrist of the main participant and then around the wrists of all the guests. The thread is worn for a minimum of three days.

The practice is performed in state ceremonies, as well as family and personal events. Some of the occasions marked are:

- death and helping relatives mourn someone who has passed over
- marriage
- birth
- going away or returning from a journey
- during festivals
- New Year
- upon entering the monkhood.

This ceremony has a deep meaning for Lao people, and is an important part of their culture.

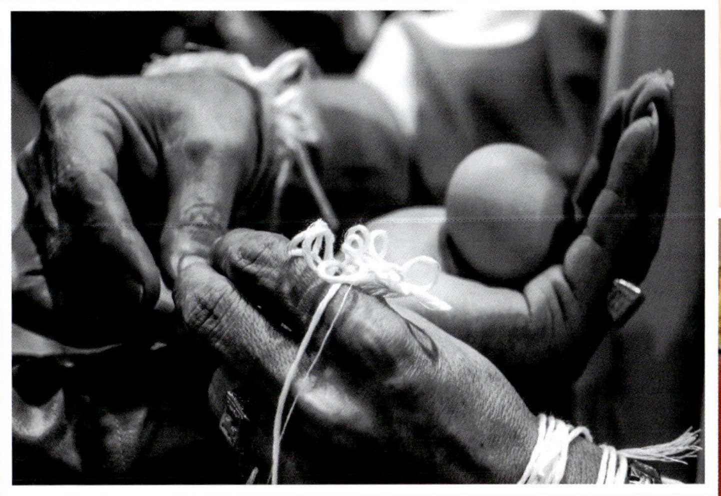

Food and Cuisine

Lao cuisine is very similar to its Northeast Thai, Vietnamese and Cambodia neighbours. *Khao niao* (sticky rice) is Laos' staple food and is eaten with every meal. It is eaten in numerous different ways, such as shaped into balls, ground and toasted, made into sweet cakes or ground to bind sausages.

Lao cuisine incorporates fresh vegetables and tropical fruits, meats and spices. Galangal, lemongrass, and *padaek* (fermented fish sauce) are important ingredients. Dishes are traditionally grilled, boiled, stewed, steamed, seared or mixed in salads. Stir-frying is now common but is considered to be of Chinese influence.

Mealtime is important in Laos. Traditionally, eating is communal, with diners sitting on a reed mat on the wooden floor around a raised platform woven out of rattan called a ka toke. Meals are eaten by hand, with spoons used for soup and chopsticks used for noodles.

Colonial Cuisine

Vientiane has several good French restaurants where baguettes and croissants are widely available, both reminders of the country's French colonial past.

On the Menu

Phor

The national dish of Vietnam, pho is known as phor in Laos and it is found everywhere. It's a noodle soup mainly eaten at breakfast, and consists of noodles, onions and slivers of chicken, pork or beef, in a beef or chicken broth.

Larb/Laap

Larb/Laap is a salad made from minced meat (raw or cooked) accompanied by a diverse assortment of vegetables, young leaves, herbs, seasoning and spice.

Sai Uah, Sai Gok

Lao-style pork sausages are essential to many Lao dishes. The pork is mixed with galangal, kaffir leaves, shallots, lemongrass, coriander, chillies and fish sauce. Some include sticky rice inside.

Khao Piak Sen

This chewy noodle soup is made with rice noodles, pork or chicken, lemongrass, galangal, shallots, garlic, chopped coriander leaves, bean sprouts and slow cooked in bone broth and served with freshly sliced limes. It is considered to be a comfort food in Laos.

Mok Pa (Steamed fish in banana leaves)

Mok pa is fish cooked with lemongrass, kaffir lime leaves, fish sauce and chillies, then wrapped up and steamed.

Geography and Climate

Laos covers 236,800 square kilometres and is located in the heart of Southeast Asia. It is landlocked with Vietnam, Cambodia, Myanmar, Thailand and China as its borders. It is a country with abundant natural resources and a wide variety of fauna and flora. Over 70% of the country is mountainous.

River Life

The western border of Laos is marked by the Mekong River, which originates in the Yunnan Province of China and travels south, forming the boundary between Laos and its neighbours. The Mekong is vitally important to Laos. Almost all other rivers eventually feed into the Mekong and strongly affect Laotian daily life. These rivers and their tributaries provide a means of transport as well as providing fertile soils for agriculture. There are over 20,000 species of plants in the Mekong area, 1,200 different kinds of bird and over 1,300 species of fish. The Mekong River is also home to the rare Irrawaddy dolphins.

Climate

Laos' tropical climate is characterised by high temperatures and humidity throughout the year. April and May feature the hottest temperatures while the weather in June sees the monsoon pattern bringing heavy rain through to October. The climate varies by region, with cooler temperatures in the mountains in the north.

Top of the World

The country's highest peak is Phou Bia at 2,819 metres.

Fabulous Flora and Fauna

Laos is well known for its rich variety of flora and fauna. Much of the country is still covered by tropical and subtropical forest. These forests are composed of three vegetation layers. High reaching dipterocarps form the top layer, while the middle canopy is made up of hardwood and the third layer consists of small bushes, shrubs, wild grasses, climbers and bamboos. Bamboo is a quick growing plant that can be farmed for many purposes such as construction, handicrafts and papermaking. Laos is home to many species of flowering bamboo.

Laos has a number of animal species that are listed as vulnerable or critically endangered. These include the Asian Elephant, Banteng, black gibbon, red panda and tiger.

About 500 species of bird are in Laos, as well as many unique amphibians, reptiles and insects. Some of the country's unusual animals are:

- Asiatic black bear
- pileated gibbon
- Irrawaddy squirrel
- Asiatic golden cat
- assamese macaque
- buff-cheek gibbon
- Francois Leaf monkey
- clouded leopard
- long-tailed goral
- Sikkim rat
- smooth-coated otter

Kuang Si Falls

Tourism and Major Sites

Tourism is growing annually, with more visitors discovering the natural wonders of Laos and its relaxed, welcoming people.

Luang Prabang

The town of Luang Prabang situated in northern Laos, was designated a UNESCO World Heritage Site in 1995. It was the ancient royal capital of the Lan Xang Kingdom and is still considered the heart of the country. This picturesque place is a mix of French colonial architecture, ancient temples and natural beauty. Located 700 metres above sea level and encircled by mountains, it is one of the country's most important tourism sites.

Pha That Luang

The most sacred monument in Laos is Pha That Luang, or the Great Stupa. This gold-covered Buddhist stupa is in the centre of Vientiane and a place of great importance to the Laos people. Its image is also on Laos' official seal.

Kuang Si Falls

The Kuang Si Falls, sometimes called Tat Kuang Si Waterfalls, is a three levelled waterfall about 29 kilometres south of Luang Prabang and one of the most beautiful natural wonders in Laos.

Imortant Sites

As of 2018, there are two UNESCO World Heritage sites in Laos, which make up the country's most important tourist destinations. Both are World Cultural Heritage Sites.

- Town of Luang Prabang (1995)
- Vat Phou and Associated Ancient Settlements within the Champasak

Nominated on the tentative list are:

- Sites Mégalithiques de la province de Xieng Khouang (1992)
- That Luang de Vientiane (1992)
- Hin Nam No National Protected Area (2016)

These sites may be listed as UNESCO World Heritage sites in the future.

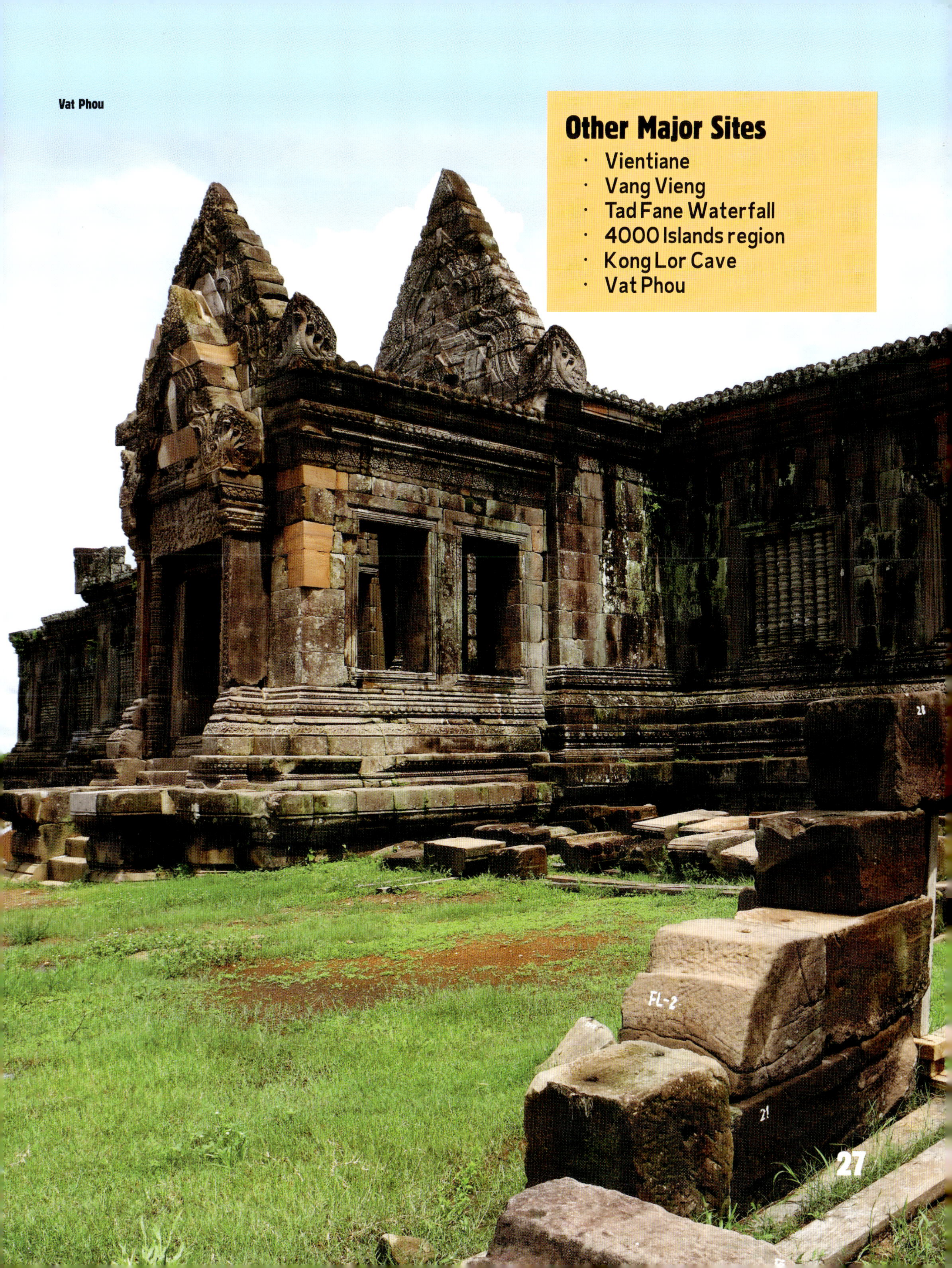

Vat Phou

Other Major Sites

- Vientiane
- Vang Vieng
- Tad Fane Waterfall
- 4000 Islands region
- Kong Lor Cave
- Vat Phou

Transport

Because Laos is a landlocked country, it has no ports or sea harbours. The Mekong provides river travel opportunities but these can be long. Rail has only developed recently, with plans for a major railway line underway. There are several modes of transport that have undergone modernisation in recent years including highways and airports, but it will take some time to reach the standards of a developed country. Many people in rural areas still travel by foot, ox-cart or pack-horse.

Road

About 80% of roads in Laos are still unpaved. A number of roads were built under French colonial rule, with more from the 1950s, which increased the movement of goods. However, it wasn't until the 1990s that more focus was given to road building and upgrading. The capital Vientiane is connected by road with other cities such as Luang Prabang, Vang Vieng and Savannakhet. New and improved roads have made it is easier for villagers to seek medical care, send children to schools and to better access work opportunities.

Connecting Countries

Laos has overland routes to its bordering neighbours, Thailand, Vietnam, Cambodia, and China, but not yet Myanmar.

Border Crossings

Vietnam: There are at least six border crossings between Laos and Vietnam.
Thailand: There are eight border crossings, including three Thai-Lao Friendship Bridges. A fourth friendship bridge opened in 2013, which links Laos, Thailand and China.
Cambodia: Due to underdeveloped roads on both sides of the border, road travel between Laos and Cambodia, while possible, is long and slow.
China: There is a major highway that connects Laos to Kunming in China.

Getting Around

Buses and trucks clog the highways. There are numerous bus companies that travel longer distances, while motorbikes and tuk tuks are used for shorter trips. Laos has become a popular country for travellers to cycle around, with excellent routes and tours available.

Highway Stats

- Laos has 21,716 kilometres of highway.
- 9,673.5 kilometres are paved.

Railways

Rail is still developing in Laos, with only a few short tracks built during French Colonial rule and one more recently connecting with Thailand. However, China is building a Pan-Asia Railway Network that will have various train lines running from Kunming (in China) to Singapore. The eastern line will run through Vietnam, Cambodia and Thailand, before heading south through Malaysia to Singapore. Laos will be a major route between China and Thailand. This high-speed railway will bring numerous economic benefits to Laos. China is responsible for 70% of the total investment, while Laos will fund 30%.

Air

Laos has over 50 airports but only nine have paved runways. Wattay International Airport is the main airport for the country. Lao Airlines is the only carrier that serves domestic routes. Thai Airways, Vietnam Airlines and Bangkok Airways serve international routes. With Laos becoming a popular tourist destination, cheap fares to destinations all over Southeast Asia are now possible.

Water Transport

Laos has about 4,587 kilometres of navigable water routes, primarily the Mekong and its tributaries. A further 3,000 kilometres of waterways is navigable to smaller boats.

Flags, Symbols and Emblems

Flag of Laos

The Laos flag has a white circle on a blue field that is said to represent the moon shining over the Mekong River. The blue stripe represents wealth and the red represents the blood shed during the internal struggle for freedom. The Laos flag was officially adopted on 2 December 1975.

National Emblem

The emblem of Laos depicts the national shrine Pha That Luang. On each side are stalks of rice. The inscriptions on the bottom read: "Peace, independence, democracy, unity and prosperity." The emblem was adopted in 1992.

National Anthem

The national anthem of the Lao People's Democratic Republic is Pheng Xat Lao (literally "Hymn of the Lao People"). It was composed by Dr Thongdy Sounthonevichit and adopted as the national anthem in 1945.

National Symbol

Indian elephant.

National Flower

Plumeria (Frangipani).

National Instrument

The Khene, which is a mouth organ made up of several pieces of bamboo.

Find Out More

Primary and Secondary Sources

A primary source is information created by someone who was a part of or witnessed the historical event first hand. Primary sources are very important to historians researching events and time periods. Examples of primary sources are letters, emails, filmed interviews and clips, journals and diaries, census statistics, government documents, art and maps (from the time period), the news (both print and film), photographs and modern maps.

A secondary source is when someone who did not actually witness the event retells the facts that someone else told them. Examples of secondary sources include news (both print and film), interviews, letters, journals and diaries, biographies, textbooks and paraphrased quotations.

Primary and Secondary Source Search

Every year, dozens of people die due to lethal remnants buried in Laos from the intensive American bombing of that country during the Vietnam War era. Can you find primary and secondary sources on this?

READ

- *Everybody Sees The Ants* by AS King
- *Moon Bear* by Gill Lewis
- *Escaping the Tiger* by Laura Manivong

Search Key Words

Laos, Mekong River, Vientiane, Luang Prabang, Vang Vieng, Tad Fane Waterfall, 4000 Islands region, Wat Phu

Glossary

BACI: an important Lao ceremonial custom
BUDDHISM: a religion based on the teachings of Buddha
CULTURE: practices, beliefs and customs of a society or people
DIALECT: a variation of a language unique to a region
ENDANGERED: when a species is at risk
ETHNIC GROUP: people who share a common culture, language and heritage
HIGHLANDS: a mountainous or elevated region
LANDMINES: explosive traps that detonate when they come into contact with a person or vehicle
MEKONG RIVER: a trans-boundary river in Southeast Asia
MONSOON: a season of heavy rain
NGO'S non-governmental organisations
PLATEAU: large, flat area found in higher regions
SUSTAINABILITY: to support the environment
TROPICAL: hot, humid climate
TYPHOON: a powerful tropical storm
UXO: unexploded ordnance

Index